Pegasus

Story by Janeen Brian
Illustrations by Meredith Thomas

⟨S⟩Harcourt Achieve

Rigby • Saxon • Steck-Vaughn

www.HarcourtAchieve.com
1.800.531.5015

Rigby PM Extensions Chapter Books
part of the Rigby PM Program
Ruby Level

Published by Harcourt Achieve Inc.
P.O. Box 27010, Austin, Texas 78755.

U.S. edition © 2005 Harcourt Achieve Inc.

First published in 2003 by Thomson Learning Australia
Pegasus © Thomson Learning Australia 2003
Illustrations © Thomson Learning Australia 2003

10 9 8 7 6 5 4 3 2 1
07 06 05 04

Printed in China by 1010 Printing Limited

Pegasus
ISBN 0 7578 9234 5

Dedicated to Amy,
with love.
From Janeen.

Contents

CHAPTER 1

The New Foal

Silently Amy named the glistening new creature Pegasus. Then she shivered. The barn was chilly in the dawn. Amy couldn't take her eyes off the slimy, leggy bundle that lay on the fresh straw. Challenge licked her newborn foal and gave a small whinny.

Zack laughed and wriggled forward. Amy immediately grabbed her younger brother's arm.

"Don't move," she whispered, more fiercely than she'd intended.

"Stop it, Amy," cried Zack, tugging his arm free. "I'm only watching."

Kneeling first, the foal tried to stand. Its thin legs buckled and wobbled and it toppled back on the straw. Amy pulled at Zack's shoulder.

"Don't go too close," she muttered out the side of her mouth. "You'll scare it."

"No I won't."

Suddenly the foal was up.

Amy caught her breath. For a moment the creature stood poised like a small, rickety table. Then it took a hesitant step, dipped its neck, and nuzzled its mother's underbelly.

Zack said to their dad, "Let's call it Star!"

Amy spun around, defiant. One look at her father, and she felt her face flare scarlet.

"Dad!" she hissed. "He can't call it Star."

CHAPTER 2

The Name of a Legend

Zack jutted his jaw. "Yes, I can. It's got a white bit on its leg and it looks like—"

"But, Dad!" Amy heard the despair in her voice. "You promised *I* could name the foal!"

In the shadows of the barn her father looked confused. "Did I?"

Amy couldn't believe it. It was the most important thing that had happened since they'd moved to the farm. "Don't, Dad," she begged. "Don't let it be Star."

"Star's good," cried Zack. Then, to Amy's annoyance, he stepped in front of her and looked squarely up at their dad. "Isn't it!"

"We'll talk about it later, kids," Dad said gently.

"Well, I'm going to call it Star."

"No," said Amy, trembling. "It's already got a name. It's called Pegasus."

Zack's mouth twisted. "Pega-*what*! That's a stupid name."

"For your information, Pegasus is the name of a wonderful horse – a horse that could fly!"

Zack clucked his tongue in disgust. "It's a *dumb* name," he grunted. Then added, "Real horses can't fly."

Amy bit her lip and turned back to look at the foal, hating her brother. She felt her father's hand on her shoulder.

"Pegasus, eh? Long time since I've heard that name," said her dad. "It's from a folktale, isn't it?"

Amy could tell her dad was trying to be nice, but why couldn't he just tell Zack that the foal wasn't going to be called Star.

"From a *legend*," Amy corrected. "A Greek legend." Even as she said it, a picture of Regan's bedroom came into her mind. She remembered the story she used to read to Regan, when her best friend could no longer read for herself.

"Yeah," nodded Dad, "that's right." He leaned on the rail and stared as the foal began to drink from its mother. Then, as a sort of afterthought, he turned toward his son and said casually, "You know, Zack, Pegasus might not be such a bad name. It might mean he'll be fast. Like he's flying."

Amy waited to see if Zack would bite. Her brother could be as stubborn as a mule at times.

Pegasus-Star

After a while, Zack gave in. "Okay," he drawled. Then he added firmly, "But his second name's Star."

Amy sighed, relieved. She didn't care what the foal's second name was. He could have five other names if Zack wanted, and it wouldn't have made any difference to her. His *real* name was Pegasus, and that's all that mattered.

After a quick glance back at Pegasus, Amy ran out of the barn and bounded up the small slope toward the house. She kicked off her boots at the back door and rushed inside, hoping her mom was awake.

"Mom!" she cried. "Mom!"

Her mother, dressed in a red bathrobe and warm slippers, was already in the kitchen cooking toast and stirring a pot of bubbling hot oatmeal. "Brrr," she said and gave a shiver. "So, how's everything going out there?"

"He's born, Mom! He's born!" Amy cried with excitement, and she wrapped her arms around her mother. "He's beautiful, *so* beautiful. And he's brown like chocolate."

Mom stroked Amy's tangled hair. "Chocolate? He sounds lovely. And how's Challenge? Is she a proud mom?"

Amy sat on the kitchen chair, eyes glistening. "You should've heard the noises Challenge made when the foal was coming out. She was so brave."

"I'll come down and have a look as soon as this cooks. Has the foal got a name yet?"

"Yeah. Pegasus." When she saw her mom's brow furrow, Amy added, "Like the special horse in the Greek legend."

Before Mom could say anything, the back door slammed.

"Zack!" Mom called, distracted. "Just *close* the door, please? And remember your boots."

Zack marched importantly into the kitchen, the collar of his pyjamas sticking out of his green sweater. "I saw the foal being born, Mom," he said.

"Amy's just been telling me. Chocolate brown, she says."

"Not *all over*," corrected Zack. "There's a white bit on his leg. Guess what it looks like, Mom?"

Mom put her hand over her mouth and covered a yawn. "I don't know, Zack."

"Guess," he insisted.

Amy rolled her eyes and spooned some sugar onto her bowl of oatmeal. "Give her a clue, Zack."

Just then Dad entered the room. He held his hands under warm water to thaw them. "Whew, it's icy out there," he said. "But everything's fine."

"Don't tell Mom what the white bit on the foal looks like, Dad." said Zack. "She's guessing." Then he quickly turned back to Mom. "It's something in the sky."

"The moon?" said Mom.

"No."

"A cloud?"

"No."

"The sun?"

"No." Zack grinned and shook his head.

Amy sensed her mom had already guessed and was only stringing Zack along.

"Give up?" Zack asked.

"Yes, I give up," said Mom.

"A star! It looks like a star. And it's just there." Zack pointed to a spot above his knee. "Star. That would've been a good name, wouldn't it, Mom?"

Amy turned swiftly. "I've told Mom already – he's called Pegasus."

"Pegasus-*Star*, you mean," Zack reminded her.

CHAPTER 4

Who's the Boss?

"So who's going to be boss of the foal?" asked Zack, as he picked up the milk carton.

"What do you mean, the boss?" asked Dad.

"You know. Who does he belong to?"

"Both of you, of course," said Dad.

"Good," said Zack. "I thought you'd say Amy could have him, just because she's older."

"How can we share a foal?" cried Amy. And, remembering her brother's lack of concentration skills, added, "What if Zack forgets the water – or forgets to feed him?"

"I wouldn't!" Zack defended hotly.

"What about those fish at our old house?" Amy accused. "You forgot to feed them. And they all died!"

Zack opened his eyes wide. Amy could see him searching for an answer. "A foal is bigger!" he said triumphantly. "I'd never forget a foal."

"I should think not," said Dad.

Amy finished chewing a piece of toast, lowered her eyes, and rested her cheek in one hand. Her mind slipped back to when they'd first arrived at the farm. She had never wanted to come. She hadn't wanted to leave their old house, to leave all her classmates and her school. Especially so soon after Regan had gone.

How she had hated the farm back then: the big, old house with its rattly windows and dark hallways; the garden plots full of weeds and overgrown trees; the stupid wandering sheep. She'd even hated Challenge.

Six months ago Mom and Dad had decided they wanted to move to a farm in the country. Every night Amy had crossed her fingers they'd change their minds.

They didn't. Moving day had been the second worst day in her life.

Now, at least, Amy knew she *liked* the

farm. But it was Pegasus that she loved. Amy knew that already. She knew it just like the first time she had met Regan.

CHAPTER 5

Getting Separated

They must have been so little then. Both in preschool. They both liked painting with the thick, yellow paint. That's how they came to be best friends.

Later they found out they also liked reading and building with blocks. In the playground, though, Regan was much braver than Amy. Once she climbed on to the classroom roof to get a football that the boys had kicked up there.

All through school, Amy and Regan did everything together. Amy never thought about what it might be like if her best friend wasn't there. Then Regan got sick. Really sick. Sometimes, when Amy arrived at school, Regan wouldn't be there. Amy would discover later she'd been at the doctor's.

"*Again*?" Amy would cry. "What's wrong?"

Regan would shrug her shoulders and say she was having special tests.

Amy would try and make her friend laugh. "Did you pass them?" she'd say.

But they never really talked about the tests or what might be wrong. Not then. Not until they couldn't ignore it any more.

23

Amy felt her shoulder being shaken.

"Amy to Earth. Come in, Amy."

Amy blinked. She stared, puzzled, at her father. "What, Dad?"

"I was saying to Zack that you'd better sort things out. Who's going to do which jobs with the foal, I mean."

Amy glanced at Zack. If only she didn't have to share Pegasus. If only Zack would agree to give up his foal-rights. One look at his jutted jaw, however, and Amy knew he wouldn't. Not yet, at any rate. Still, she thought, no harm trying.

"How about Zack looks after Challenge," she began, "and I—"

Zack shot her a look. "No way, Amy. Just because you want the foal to yourself. Well, you can't have him. He's half mine and when he's older I'm going to train him and win races and everything."

"But you don't even like horses, Zack."

"I *do*!"

"Well, how come you never spend much time with Challenge? You hardly ever want to ride *her*?"

"I don't have to!" he countered. "But I'll ride Pegasus-Star. You'll see."

"All I can see," said Mom, pulling her bathrobe tight around her, "is two lucky kids who are arguing over nothing. Now, Zack, go and get dressed. And, Amy—"

Amy stood without having to be told. She cleared her dishes then walked to her bedroom. The first thing she looked at was Regan's photo. It was in a blue china frame with yellow fish painted on it. It reminded Amy of how much Regan used to love going to the beach.

Amy sunk onto her bed, the frame in her hands, and thought some more about her best friend. In the end, Regan and the girl in the photo could've been two totally different people. As the cancer had worsened, Regan had grown short of breath. Then her uniform looked like it'd been made for someone twice her size. Eventually, she had been too sick even to go to school.

Then Amy used to ride round to her place after school. Regan's face would light up – she was always so happy to see Amy. But she'd either be in bed or in a big lounge chair with pillows all around her. And everything smelled of medicines.

Regan wanted to know what was happening at school and what all the kids were doing. Amy would tell her everything she could remember. Sometimes she'd even make up stories, just to see Regan smile.

Then came the time when Regan could no longer see. That afternoon, when Amy arrived, she saw the tears trickle down Regan's cheeks. Amy hugged her friend hard. Her stomach tightened and there was a burning behind her eyes, but she didn't cry. Instead she read to Regan. Regan had a book of Greek legends. Many, many times, in the afternoons that followed, Amy read the story about the beautiful horse that could fly. It was Regan's favorite.

Two months later Regan died.

CHAPTER **6**

Let's Run

Amy wiped some dust from the frame and set it back on her night stand.

She could hear Zack in his bedroom. He was jumping about and making loud shooting sounds with his mouth. Amy got up and shut her door. Then she got dressed and pulled on the familiar blue sweater that smelled of Challenge.

They hadn't been at the farm long, Amy remembered, when she and her parents had had a big fight. Amy had yelled. She'd said she hated the place and as soon as she was old enough she was going to leave and go back to her *real* home. Then she'd stormed down the slope, past the barn and the river and, dry-eyed, hit her fists on a railing post.

Then she'd heard a soft snicker. Challenge had padded up behind her. Gently, the horse had leaned her head on Amy's shoulder and nuzzled her neck above the sweater band. At that moment, something had snapped inside Amy. Her body just let go and she began to cry. With her arms around Challenge's neck and her head pressed into the horse's warm coat, Amy had cried until she could cry no more.

This was the same sweater that Amy was wearing now. She felt comfortable in it. She felt safe.

Amy brushed her hair, tied it back, and headed toward the kitchen.

"Come and see Pegasus, Mom," she said.

Mom and Amy linked arms and walked together down the slope toward the barn. "Wait till you see him," Amy sighed. "He's so beautiful."

"Amy," Mom began, and rested her warm palm over the back of Amy's hand, "you know what Zack's like." She paused.

Amy thought she understood what her mother meant. That, in time, Zack would lose interest in the foal. He'd go off hunting frogs, chasing lizards, climbing trees, or whatever, and Amy would be left to care for the foal.

She relaxed, happy and content. In her mind, Amy saw herself watching the foal grow, looking after him, and whispering the name that would always remind her of Regan.

Suddenly Amy swung around and grabbed both her mother's hands. "Come on!" she urged, laughing at her mom's surprise. "Let's run! I want you to see Pegasus!"